DOGOLOGY

DOGOLOGY

(What your dog is *really* thinking)

FELIX OSBORNE

SIRIUS

SIRIUS

This edition published in 2022 by Sirius Publishing, a division of
Arcturus Publishing Limited,
26/27 Bickels Yard, 151–153 Bermondsey Street,
London SE1 3HA

Text and illustrations © Noodle Fuel Ltd 2022
Illustrations by Jade Orlando 2022

ISBN: 978-1-3988-2071-5
AD007515UK

Printed in China

When the Man waked up he said,
'What is Wild Dog doing here?'

And the Woman said,
'His name is not Wild Dog any more,
but the First Friend, because he
will be our friend for always
and always and always.'

Rudyard Kipling, *The Jungle Book*

Acknowledgements

Thanks to Chewie, our
Irish Doodle, for being the
inspiration for this book.

Contents

From a dog's perspective...

Humans have shared their world with dogs since their ancestors first tamed wolves – our ancestors – with the warmth of their fires, and the scraps from their plates. However, in order to make this complicated relationship with humans work, dogs have developed a sophisticated set of rules. Each of these rules is designed to make sure that humans understand exactly what is expected of them. This ensures that dogs, as a species, are kept in the comfort we deserve.

This guide to what we are really thinking takes humans through the different elements of our dogtastic world to show just how far-reaching canine influence has become.

Dog breeds are a good example of this. As homes and houses became smaller, some larger dog breeds were no longer suitable for domestic spaces. In response, we developed smaller versions of ourselves – lapdogs or the 'handbag' breeds. Teacup poodles, miniature dachshunds and Chihuahuas became incredibly popular especially for humans living in city apartments.

As a solution to more and more people becoming allergic to us, a new breed was developed. The poodle cross took advantage of the poodle's hypoallergenic and non-shedding coat. The poodle cross soon became very sought-after. Its sister breed – the cross poodle – was considerably less successful due to its irritability. You now can't move in suburbia for cockapoos, cavapoos, or labradoodles as owners simultaneously love their pet's soft fur and the fact that it doesn't coat their carpets.

Gasp in amazement at the secret meaning behind our interactions with humans and other animals, especially squirrels. Understand the complex nature of our daily routine and the importance of poo in that ritual. Prepare to be astonished by the role canines have played in history and literature, as well as the impact we have had on the human world around us.

But above all, relish this opportunity to spend some time with your most faithful friends and finally answer the question of just who's looking after who.

We give you – the dog!

Dogs:
The Basics

What is a Dog?

Okay, so we're going to start with the very basics...

The dictionary definition of a dog is

a domesticated carnivorous mammal that typically has a long snout, an acute sense of smell, non-retractable claws, and a barking, howling, or whining voice.

We think that glosses over some of our most important characteristics. When choosing your doggy companion, it's important to make sure you know about the temperament of the canine you're considering. There's more to it than size, looks or the amount of exercise we need.

Turn the page to gain an insight into some of the more unusual ways to select a dog to share your home!

Fluffy dogs

These cute little dogs have everybody fooled. The Pomeranian, the Bichon frisé or the Lhasa apso, are actually ninjas in disguise, ready to pounce at a moment's notice. Watch out, humans!

Big dogs

The Great Dane, or the Irish wolfhound can seem a bit of a handful due to their size. Be careful, as they can use their height to access forbidden places.

Anti-allergy dogs

The poodle cross has created many options for
those looking for hypo-allergenic hounds – just
be careful which size poodle you choose!

Second-hand dogs

Sadly the need for rescue homes for dogs hasn't gone away,
but they can be a good place to find an older member
of the canine fraternity who is already house-trained.

Working dogs

Traditional working breeds such as the border collie or American Akita have long been in awe of the hard and sometimes painful hours put in by the so-called family pet.

Looks exhausting!

Powerful dogs

Rottweilers and Dobermans are often chosen by humans for their supposedly intimidating characteristics, but the dark secret of both breeds is that they have a secret shared love of knitting.

Fashion conscious dogs

The poodle and French bulldog take their appearance seriously, ensuring they accessorize to match their owners' outfits at all times.

If you think I'm going out with you dressed like that, you can think again!

The Mutt

The enduring mongrel – jack of all breeds, master of none – no pedigree, no hybrid cross, just a friendly honest dog! And our best-loved!

Puppy Rules

It's very exciting to be a puppy. For a certain amount of time, you will be forgiven for any misdemeanour due to your extreme cuteness. As such, you have your own set of rules to allow you to exploit human forgiveness to its maximum potential while you are still cute enough to get away with it.

Puppy Rule 1

When in the wrong, **OPEN YOUR EYES** as wide as possible. You will immediately be forgiven. Bottom lip quiver optional, usually unnecessary.

Puppy Rule 2

Your teeth are the sharpest they will ever be, **USE THEM** on everything you can – humans, food, furniture, anything...

Puppy Rule 3

Take advantage of **YOUR SIZE** – if you can squeeze behind a sofa, DO! If you can tunnel under the sideboard, HAVE AT IT! Your owner will be filled with pride and joy.

Puppy Rule 4

TREATS will fall like manna from heaven. The treat rate slows as you get older, so make the most of it.

Puppy Rule 5

Toilet training is **BORING**... but it is fun to see
how many times you can make a human stand up
and take you outside before they get annoyed.

Puppy Rule 6

If **NERVOUS**, sit on your owner's feet. This means they
can't get away and will often pick you up for cuddles.

Puppy Rule 7

Like treats, you can never have too many **CUDDLES**.

Puppy Rule 8

Small humans can be **UNPREDICTABLE**. Limit
interaction with them unless they are part of your pack.

Puppy Rule 9

If you share a house with a **CAT**, understand
that you should respect them at all times and you
should only lick them when specifically invited.

Puppy Rule 10

Own your **CUTENESS** or it will own you
– remember, this is your superpower.

In the Prime of Life

At this stage of your life, you will be in charge of the household. You should have trained your humans to ensure that they deliver the four key elements of your life.

1. Food

2. Walkies

3. Sleep

4. Tummy rubs

In the Slow Lane

As you get older things get a little bit tricky. You don't have as much energy. Your eyesight is suffering, it takes longer to get out of bed in a morning, but in your dreams you're still bounding across fields chasing rabbits.

We all suffer the indignity of old age. Joints creak, digestion isn't what it used to be, but tummy rubs are still a very good thing!

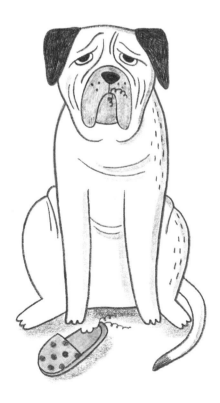

Ten Rules of Dog Ownership as written by Dogs

1. There is no such thing as **ENOUGH** treats.

2. All kitchen work surfaces should be no more than one foot off the ground.

3. The bark alarm is both useful and informative and should be encouraged at all times.

4. Pee-mail should be checked regularly and thoroughly on every walk.

5. Any soft horizontal surface is, by definition, a **BED** – this includes sleeping humans.

6. Toys are a necessity and are not optional.

7. The dishwasher is an acceptable source of food.

8. The dog groomer is **NOT** a nice person.

9. We are fully aware that V. E. T. spells 'vet'.

10. See rule one.

Dog Names by Dogs

Names as bestowed by humans	What dogs actually call themselves...
Fifi	Arterielle, Warrior Princess
Trixie	Boudicca, Digger of Holes and Queen of the Chase
Flash	He Who Runs with Rabbits
Buster	Clint Growl, International Dog of Mystery
Rascal	Snarls Barkley

Muffin	**Sir Growly Woofington**
Duke	**Duchess**
Barney	**Ludovic, Star of the Opera**
Rufus	**Bark Fury, Devourer of Fox Poo**
Biscuit	**She Who Snatches**
Shadow	**Kevin**

The Stinky Shame

**As a dog you'll quickly discover that humans
have an unhealthy obsession with what
comes from our nether regions.**

After hovering awkwardly nearby, waiting for us to do
our business, they then pick it up! Humans are weird!

What Dog Poop Actually Means

1. Normal healthy diet

2. Dehydrated / running at speed

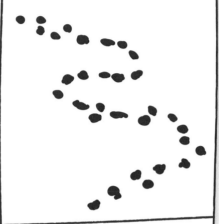

3. I probably shouldn't have eaten that.

4. I hate you, human! / tummy bug

A Dog's Daily Routine

The Most Important Thing in a Dog's Life

Dogs spend a lot of time thinking about food.

Our day is punctuated by small moments of delight when food is placed in front of us. It looks something like this.

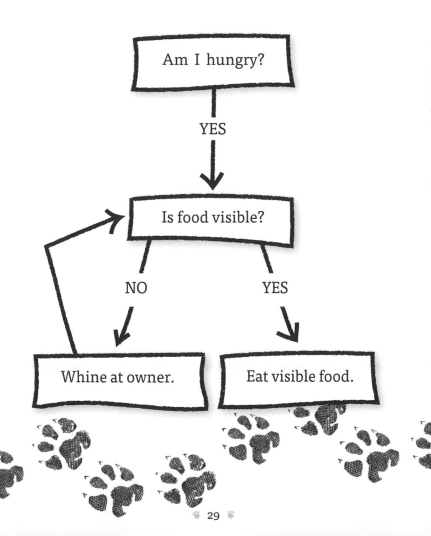

The Second Most Important Thing in a Dog's Life

Humans often make the mistake of assuming that because their dog has eaten their own bodyweight in kibble, that they will no longer be hungry. This brings us neatly back to the subject of treats.

Dogs understand that food doesn't count as treats and treats don't count as food.

Through a strange quirk of fate, all of the most delicious treats start with 'CH'.

CHicken

CHeese

CHurkey

*There is a fourth CH treat – but it is forbidden. It's called CHocolate and smells divine. We aren't allowed to eat it though as it makes us sick.

...and on the eighth day God created

~~CHeanut~~ Peanut Butter

**Here are the mystical techniques for summoning
this heavenly substance into being.**

Make it extremely difficult for your owner to groom you.

Tap dance when your owner is trying to clip your claws.

Rush around madly while your owner and
their pack are trying to watch TV.

As a reward for your efforts your owner may put some
miracle butter inside a toy for you to excavate, and
sometimes, they may even spread some of the delicious
elixir on their forehead for you to lick*. Worryingly this
is not the strangest thing you will see your human do.

Google it.

The Third Most Important Thing in a Dog's Life

Once they have ensured that our food and treat requirements have been met to our satisfaction, our owner's next most important task is showering us with the requisite level of adoration.

The best ways for dog owners to demonstrate their overwhelming love for us is to slowly and carefully work their way through this preprepared list.

1. Basic tummy rub.

2. Ear tickle.

3. Head scratch.

4. Downward-facing dog tummy rub*.

5. Flank stroke.

6. Upward-facing dog tummy rub*.

7. Double ear tickle.

8. Whole body cuddle**.

* *humans sometimes do this while breathing heavily. Ignore them, they're just being weird.*

** *may or may not be possible based on size of dog.*

If the owner is distracted, or hasn't been paying sufficient attention to their dog, we clever hounds have an unrivalled method of ensuring our owner's obedience.

Tactical Deployment of Prone Dog Position

1. Roll onto back.

2. Spread legs akimbo.

3. Stretch out front legs.

4. Let front paws drop appealingly.

5. Tilt head to one side.

Let Me Sing You the Song of My People

Dogs have a great variety of sounds they use when communicating with and entertaining humans.

Level 1. Almost ultra-sonic whine

This is for when we are trying to draw our human's attention to something when we really know we should be quiet – normally as a prelude to level 2.

Level 2. Audible whine

A show of distress or excitement – we could be hungry, thirsty, need to go out or want to be the other side of a door.

Level 3. Echo yip

A short, high-pitched, mid-volume bark, designed to test for proximity to humans, or as a prelude to level 5. Sometimes known as dog sonar.

Level 4: Dog Opera

Incorrectly called 'howling' by humans, a melodious continuous whine is used to attract the owner's attention when being ignored and communicate with distant brethen.

Level 5. Growl

A low sound from the back of the throat used to warn humans, other dogs, and cats especially, to think *very* carefully about their next move.

Level 6. Bark

A loud, mid-pitched noise, often repeated in threes, multiple times. It can be used to alert the owner to deliveries, ghosts and spiders. It is also necessary to stop squirrels from claiming any more territory in the garden.

Level 7. Roar

A continuous, low-pitched, very loud bark, mainly produced when the human hasn't responded properly to Level 5, or if threat has moved to Woof Con 1. Also used when human is using the vacuum cleaner.

Dogs Just Want to Have Fun

From puppyhood onwards, we dogs have a deep understanding of the importance of play.

A wise dog once said that, 'One does not stop chasing the stick because one grows old, one grows old because one stops chasing the stick.'

Most of us master the art of *the chase* and *tug of war*. Some never quite manage the finer art of *fetch*.

Basic Play: The Chase

Following a fast-moving object – ball, stick, toy, cat or squirrel – in order to capture said object.

Intermediate Play: Tug of War

When you refuse to give the fast-moving object back to owner. Sometimes your human may offer a treat as a reward for letting go. This is a good habit to encourage.

Advanced Play: Fetch

Returning the fast-moving object to your human in order for it to be thrown again for you to chase.
(See Basic Play: The Chase – doesn't apply to cat or squirrel)

Squirrel Patrol

It is very important for a dog to make sure that their home is protected at all times from squirrels. To do this, dogs the world over have formed a strategic unit called PAWS – Pups Against Worldwide Squirrels.

To become a member of PAWS, a dog must be able to carry out the following basic duties:

1. Stand guard silently for long periods of time. The hound also serves, who watches and waits.

2. On target acquisition, launch oneself at high velocity towards the enemy, forcing them to retreat to higher ground. If the enemy does not do this, we can't be responsible for our actions.

3. Bark loudly, reprimanding said critters, reminding them of their fate should they dare to ever set foot on the ground again.

4. Trot back to guard position, congratulating oneself on a job well done.

The Power of Dog Naps

Dogs can take naps in the most awkward positions. Remember we often sleep with one eye open.

The 'I know you're there' nap

The 'Please can you turn on the heating' nap

The 'You're going to have to sit somewhere else' nap

The 'If I fit, I sit' nap

The 'I've fallen and I can't get up' nap

The 'Let it all hang out' nap

Princess' Bedtime Routine

Her Last Pee

What do you mean you need me to go out?

I don't want to go out.
I really don't want to go out.

Nope, not me. Not gonna go out there.

Absolutely, definitely, I do not want a pee.

Princess And The Pea

My bed is rotated at 90 degrees, I'm not going to
lie in it until you've corrected this glaring error.

I know it's perfectly circular, but that's not the point.

Blanket and Toys

Where's my toy? No, not that toy.
Not that one either. Yes, that one!

Erm... You know I said I *didn't* need a pee...

Dogs Indoors

Where owners think dogs sit when they're out

Where we actually sit

Are you lonesome tonight?

Dogs are very loyal creatures.

Apart from experiencing a moment of existentialist dread every time our human goes out the front door, we will wait patiently for them to return, secure in our faith that humans will materialize just in time for tea.

A dog will wait.

And wait.

We might sigh.

And wait.

Until the human returns to their primary duty, which is obviously to provide us with food and affection.

Public Enemy Number 1

**While the front door can bring great
joy, it can also bring danger.**

There is a particular breed of human that insists on
attacking the house by delivering parcels. It's important
to make sure that whoever is knocking knows that there
is a fearsome hound on the other side of the door.

Types of Knock

1. Tentative, as if uncertain of response.

2. Confident. Aware that I will answer the door
and will probably be pleased to see me.

3. Knock and run. My role is to let everyone in the house know that their delivery is here.

4. Agressive, loud banging that only serves to wake up the savage beast inside.

Public Enemy Number 2

**Another worrying individual comes to the house
and attacks the windows with long poles.**

It is our duty to follow those poles up and down
whilst alerting our humans to the attack.

Their second dastardly technique is to spray some
form of liquid at the house too. I fear they may be
marking their territory the way I do on a walk.

The final iniquity is the bit where a bright yellow cloth,
squeaking against the window, is used to deploy a sonic
attack designed to disable the hearing of any dogs inside.

Our only hope is to frighten this person away
with ceaseless barking at Level 6.

Public Enemy Number 3

Other humans also come to the front door.

Some come bearing amazing-smelling boxes that we are very rarely allowed to safety test when they come through the front door. Don't they know we're only trying to ensure high standards of health and safety?

The Dreaded Bath

One should always remember that humans are nose-blind and therefore incapable of recognizing the true wonder of our divine aroma. They sometimes even resort to the barbarity of immersing us in warm water. They call this terrible experience a bath.

Some of us are small enough to fit into the kitchen sink. Humans should be careful to match the facilities to their dog.

Once we have been captured, humans use a jug or even worse, a machine called a shower to try and drown us.

They then apply a foul-smelling substance called sham-poo, which as its name implies, smells nothing like fox poo, one of nature's great fragrances.

The final stage is to rinse off and towel dry. This seems foolish to us when we have a perfectly good patented 'shake and dry' system that allows us to share the remnants of the bath with our human.

It's All Fun and Games until...

There are certain moments in every dog's life where things can take an unexpected turn for the worse.

Provoking a small dog with an aggressive large dog attitude may well result in injury. Bear in mind that small dogs don't usually need to be provoked...

A sock that smelled delicious going in, might not smell so good on its way out.

An entire trifle is not designed to be wolfed down in one sitting by one dog.

Engaging with feline claws might mean puncture wounds dripping in blood.

Any and all of the above will result in a trip to the

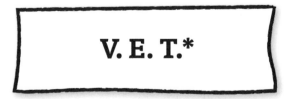

V. E. T.*

and that's never good! It might even result in... THE CONE.

*which stands for VERY
EXTREME TERROR.*

A Day Trip to the Vet

1. The journey

2. The waiting room

3. The vet

4. The examination

5. The needle

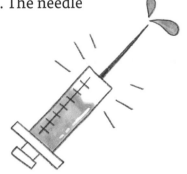

6. The **CONE** of **SHAME**

The Dog Groomer

The dog groomer is a species of human that we dogs fear even beyond the V.E.T.

In one fell swoop, a seemingly-friendly human can subject a pooch to...

horrendous water torture,

frighteningly sharp scissors,

and even more terrifying, clippers.

And all in the name of vanity – and sometimes cleanliness.

The final injustice is the application of something called 'scent' which will make a hound smell, temporarily, just as bad as a human.

Our preferred *parfum*, as all dogs recognize, is something stinky we found outside next to the bin.

When Trees Come Indoors...

Once a year, the humans do something really, really strange. They choose to bring a large, green tree inside and decorate it with pretty sparkles that we're not allowed to touch. We're not quite sure why!

Humans often get quite cross when putting the tree up. They curse at the long windy rope that lights up, but never want our assistance to bite through the knotted strings. When we offer to help, we get shouted at.

The best bit about this time of year is that the house smells of CHurkey for an entire week.

CHurkey is a much superior form of CHicken. Not only does it smell even more delicious, it is at least FOUR TIMES the size!!!

Humans often have left-over CHurkey – although we're not 100% clear how that is possible – so they put it in the magic cold box [fridge] and bring it out again later. Extra CHurkey opportunities are always a good thing.

The Outdoor Dog

Walkies

While humans consider a walk a good way to exercise us and make sure that we are healthy, there are several critical elements of our perambulations of which our owners are completely unaware.

1. Pee-mail

How else do you think we communicate with our friends in the neighbourhood? To you it's a grass verge, to us it's a message board.

2. Treats

Walks are another opportunity for treats, as you may be rewarded for good behaviour. Of course, an unscrupulous hound knows that deliberate bad behaviour can also be 'solved' with a treat...

3. Scout the Neighbourhood

Identify and assess potential threats in your immediate surroundings. A feline ambush can come from any direction at any time.

4. Meet Friends or Enemies

Sometimes you meet other pooches – this can be a good or bad thing (see pages 77–79).

5. When Unleashed

Oh the joy, the freedom, the sniffing... Small furry creatures cower at our ability to run and run and run.

Off the Lead...

Being allowed to run off the lead is a wonderful experience for us dogs. Don't worry, your human shouldn't wander too far while they are unsupervised.

However, sometimes the excitement of running in a park, or field, or on a trail can go to a dog's head and we forget the training that has been drilled into us since pup stage.

At that point, our humans may become shrill and increasingly loud, often getting irritated. It is because they are frightened and nervous and need us to lead them to the next waypoint.

Human Methods of Recall

1. Normal call sound – often our name or a short whistle. A swift return here often results in a 'good dog' or a small treat.

2. More insistent call sound – repeated high pitched initial syllable of our name. At this point, we are often further away, so it is hard to hear. A return here may get a pat, but is less likely to produce treats.

3. Urgent call sound – very loud bellow of our name in the lower register with the words, 'Come here, you little ****!' often added. This is for when humans are very anxious or even angry with us. We have strayed too far and they may fear they are in danger. Return to reassure them, treats highly unlikely.

The Power of the Nose

A dog's nose is a wonderful thing. It can tell us so much about our surroundings. When CHicken or CHeese have been taken out of the cold box, for example.

Or which of our many acquaintances have passed by the lamppost on the corner.

Our humans have very distinct smells – we don't really like it when they cover those smells with soap or things from smelly bottles. They don't understand that if they've not stood naked in the shower for two days, they smell wonderful.

Key Smelling Stops for Dogs

1. Lamppost

2. Bush

3. Bus Shelter

4. Poop Bin

The Power of our Ears

Our hearing is extremely useful. For example, being able to hear the delivery van from half a mile away allows us to alert our humans, giving them plenty of time to prepare for its arrival.

We're not keen on certain sounds: fireworks, crackly noises which might be a fire, and hissing noises which might be a cat. Sometimes we need to leave the area. This is not because we're frightened, it's because we need to check other areas... for other noises.

There is a strange condition that all dogs suffer from that we do not fully understand. When we are very excited, we suddenly lose all ability to hear our humans. (see page 62).

This condition can be cured by the simple application of treats.

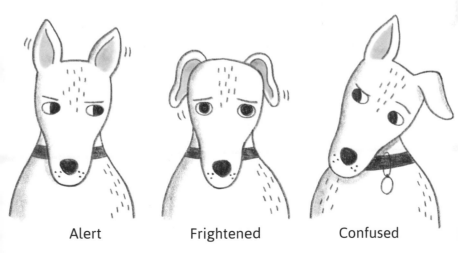

Alert   Frightened   Confused

Dogs with Jobs

Dead Bird Fetchers

These dogs are still an impressive group. They have trained their ears to ignore loud bangs and retrieve all sorts of interesting potential food sources without giving into their canine instincts at any point. Well done!

Underground Heroes

Small and nimble, these wiry hounds disappear down holes very few self-respecting pooches would choose to submit themselves to. In these deep, dark holes, these heroes often come face-to-face with scary vermin. Rather them than us.

Supersniffers

Useful at airports, rock concerts and other large venues where humans congregate. Sniffer dogs are the wine tasters of the canine world, delicately assessing the 3.5 million scents they are subjected to in order to find forbidden smells. There are much more interesting sniffs, you know, like fox poo.

Herding Hounds

There is nothing more pleasurable than herding a flock of sheep or cattle, even when the stupid creatures decide to go the other way. There are even competitions to enter to demonstrate your skill. What is even more impressive is that these dogs perform these difficult tasks while their humans stand around whistling for no readily apparent reason.

Kind Canines

While all humans need looking after, some need more help than others. A sensible and steady dog is called for in this role. It takes lots of training before a guide dog is fully able to support their owner. Some dog breeds are more suitable than others to this particular role. Chihuahua or dachshund – this may not be for you!

Rescue Rovers

Similarly, only certain breeds are able to take on the role of a rescue dog. They need a keen sense of smell, to be well-disciplined in their training, and intelligent, as well as being able to carry a hip flask around their neck. Sometimes humans don't half get themselves in a fix.

At the Dog Show

There are occasions when our humans like to show us off in all our glory.

At this point, it is fruitless to argue.

You will be subjected to the undignified process of beautification: endless baths, grooming, trimming and tooth-brushing.

In some instances, you might even be called upon to wear a 'ribbon' in your topknot.

You will have to demonstrate your abilities in recall, walking to heel and staying in one place.

This is hell.

Now is not the time to follow your owner around begging for treats, leaping up at their clothes or pulling them off their feet whilst on the lead.

We can guarantee it won't end well.

The Awesome Agility Course

Some super-smart dogs can often be found demonstrating their superior skills by competing on the agility course. No, we don't know why humans invented this either.

1. Balancing

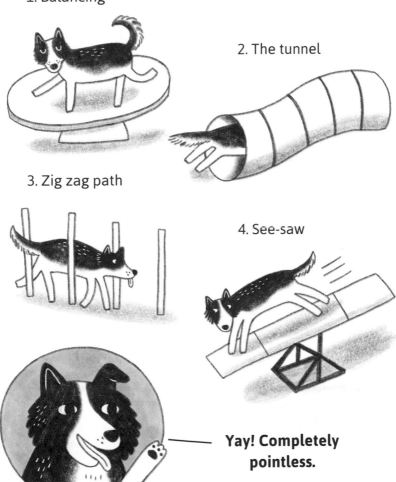

2. The tunnel

3. Zig zag path

4. See-saw

Yay! Completely pointless.

Ruff Mudder

Mud is a divisive issue for dogs. Some dogs love being out in all weathers, romping through fields of mud and then running up to their humans and planting their paws as high up their owner as they can reach*. Others are less keen and may even tiptoe around puddles.

However we feel about muddy puddles, our owners have many different methods for preventing that mud being transferred onto floors, carpets or furniture. Some are more pleasurable than others.

1. Simple Towel Rub

This is normally deployed when our paws are wet, but not muddy, and if you play your cards right, can turn into a tug of war game.

*Beware of doing this too often if you're a mid-sized dog and your human owner is male – It can have painful consequences!

2. Bucket of Water

For muddy paws, but where no mud has transferred
its way up onto your tummy or nether regions.
The longer-legged you are, the more frequently
the bucket is applied. For short-legged or smaller
dogs, you might end up in the bucket.

3. Outdoor Hose Pipe

This human method of torture is deployed when over 30%
of your surface area is covered in mud. The tap indoors can
produce warm water. The tap outdoors does not, so prepare
to freeze. Appropriate retaliation is to apply the patented
'shake and dry' method, preferably all over your owner.

4. The Dreaded Bath

For when you are beyond redemption and nothing
else will do. Abandon hope, all ye who enter here.

The Big Wet

Like mud, the big wet, which humans call the sea or the ocean, can also be divisive. For larger dogs who are strong enough to brave the waves, it can be a wonderfully refreshing romp. For smaller dogs, and those of a more timid disposition, it's safer to stay on the beach.

Beach Benefits

1. Plenty of opportunities for helping humans to finish unsupervized snacks. Especially if the beach is busy.

2. Lots of space to run and run and run. But don't, whatever you do, quench your thirst with the water from the ocean. It tastes DISGUSTING.

3. Large piles of smelly seaweed to roll around in. It must be good for us, as humans put it on their faces.

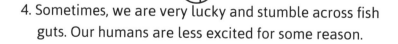

4. Sometimes, we are very lucky and stumble across fish guts. Our humans are less excited for some reason.

5. ICECREAM is exactly as delicious as it sounds, especially when licked off the floor. In extreme cases, scaring small children to make them drop their icecream is appropriate.

6. Lots of sandcastles for us to post our pee-mails on.

7. Opportunities for us to easily dig and bury our treasures. Some humans like to be buried in sand by their small humans. We like to help.

8. Some agile dogs have learned to surf. Needless to say, they are supreme operatives and heroes amongst their peers.

9. The doggy paddle is named after us for a reason. We are dogs and we paddle.

10. There is only one downside to the seaside experience, and that's the bath we have to have when we get home.

Snow Dogs

When it gets very cold, fluffy white stuff falls from the sky. Humans call it 'snow', we call it 'cold, fluffy white stuff'.

Snow adds a different dimension to the whole outdoor experience for a dog. Suddenly our pee-mails become visible, scents are covered up and squirrels and their friends stay in their homes.

Snow is also very cold. Cold on our paws, cold on our noses and definitely cold in the mouth, although it does taste better than the big wet.

For those of us with longer fur, snow can make life a little tricky. It clumps together and gets stuck in our paws – these then need to be melted onto your human's couch next to a warm fire.

Humans sometimes use dogs to pull sledges through the cold white stuff. It is a novel experience but not one we would recommend for long journeys.

Humans also make balls out of cold white stuff and throw them at each other! We are not quite sure why they do this. Balls are only supposed to be used for *chase* or *fetch*.

They build strange statues of themselves out of the cold white stuff, adding hats and scarfs to keep the cold white stuff warm. Humans are weird – it's official.

Dogs and Other Animals

Dogs, Dogs and More Dogs

There is a certain social etiquette involved when dogs meet other dogs, which doesn't just involve sniffing one another's bottom (although that is clearly extremely important).

Obviously, in our own homes, we are lord and master, but it is also contingent upon you to accept that this may not be the case in a house that belongs to another dog.

If we're on neutral territory, then there are even more unwritten rules to obey, which are both complicated and confusing.

The Rules of Engagement – in our home

We are top dog in this space, it is our home and we call the shots.

The Rules of Engagement – in another dog's home

We are beta in this space (yes, even if the dog is a quarter of your size) and so it is our role to be as polite and deferential as possible. Our humans don't like it when we embarrass them by humping the host, canine or human, so we must try to suppress our instincts and do our very best to behave.

The Rules of Engagement for Neutral Territory

These are complex rules that depend on your familiarity with the dogs you meet, and your respective sizes.

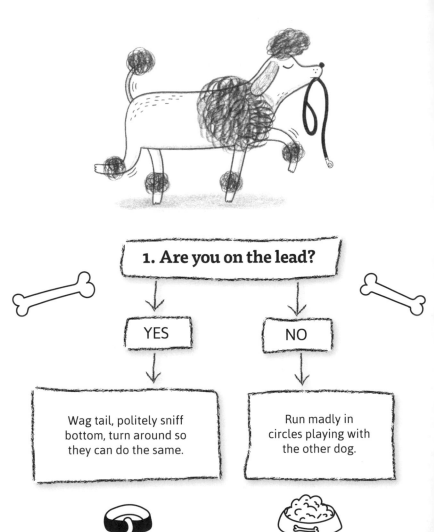

1. Are you on the lead?

YES

Wag tail, politely sniff bottom, turn around so they can do the same.

NO

Run madly in circles playing with the other dog.

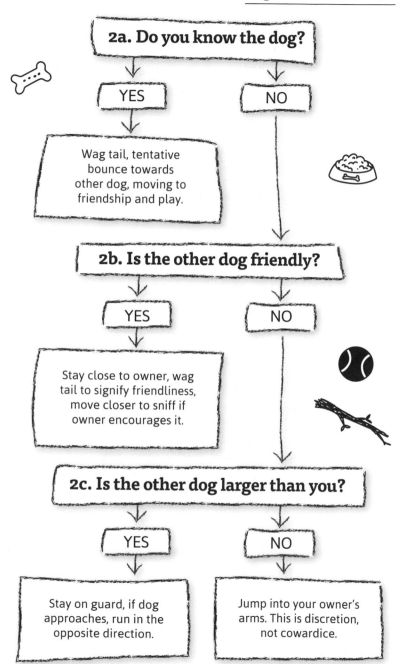

2a. Do you know the dog?

YES

NO

Wag tail, tentative bounce towards other dog, moving to friendship and play.

2b. Is the other dog friendly?

YES

NO

Stay close to owner, wag tail to signify friendliness, move closer to sniff if owner encourages it.

2c. Is the other dog larger than you?

YES

NO

Stay on guard, if dog approaches, run in the opposite direction.

Jump into your owner's arms. This is discretion, not cowardice.

Dogs ARE Wolves

Dogs are extremely proud of our wolf heritage and occasionally revert to our ancestral behaviour in moments of stress or excitement.

This is the point where we become members of...

WOLF SQUAD

All dogs are honorary members of WOLF SQUAD, but don't necessarily demonstrate those skills on a daily basis. In our world, belonging to WOLF SQUAD means taking on the mantle of the dire-wolf, our now sadly-extinct prehistoric ancestor. So there are certain rules a dog should follow to try to make sure that we don't embarrass our wild forefathers.

1. Walk tall and proud. (Even if you're a Bassett hound who doesn't have much ground clearance.)

2. Always hold your head up high to catch the scents of the wild on the wind. (Pugs – remember your snout is as big as you believe it is.)

3. Move at a stately pace, but always be a coiled
spring, ready to leap into action at a moment's notice.
(Terriers – we know you have some issues
with the whole stately pace thing, but you've
nailed the 'ready to spring' element!)

4. Use your howl sparingly, but
always join in with the chorus.
(This may seem like it will need practice, but trust
us, your wolfy instincts will always kick in.)

5. Always look after the pack.
(Whether that's other members of Wolf Squad,
or your humans, the pack is everything.)

Dogs and Cats

Dogs and cats have spent eons ensuring that the fragile balance of power is maintained.

Yes, that's right. The cat is unequivocally in charge. Why? Because they *will* hurt you.

No matter what we do, or what we would like to happen, their retractable (and therefore, perpetually razor-sharp) claws give them a distinct tactical advantage over the humble dog.

Claws have not only given these furry creatures an edge when it comes to evading capture (so they can scale things like curtains, trees, humans etc.), but they are also perfectly capable of drawing blood with a lightning-fast slash of the paw.

Mostly, dogs are satisfied with barking loudly whenever we see a feline, with an occasional half-hearted attempt to chase or catch one – just to keep up appearances. If the cat doesn't run away when you bark at it, we strongly advise you don't approach that cat.

However, in some instances, where owners have decided to introduce an element of risk into their lives, dogs and cats can live in uneasy harmony, provided of course, that the dog remembers his place in the hierarchy*.

licking the cat's behind, but only once the dog has mastered the rules on the opposite page.

Interpreting Cat Behaviour

Dogs have a finely-tuned instinct regarding our centuries-old enemy and know exactly how to work out whether we are in any real danger.

1. Cat sleeping: ready to attack, highly dangerous.

2. Cat hissing and spitting: do not approach under any circumstances, highly dangerous.

3. Cat purring: might allow possible contact for ear licking, highly dangerous.

4. Cat eating: do not even attempt to taste their food, highly dangerous.

5. Cat hunting: might allow dog to eat entrails of victim, highly dangerous.

6. Cat playing: can change to option 2 in an instant – stay alert, highly dangerous.

Emotions

Dog   ## Cat

happy

sad

friendly

enthusiastic

hungry

THIS IS A CAT TAKEOVER

Hello! It's us, the cats. We've had enough of this. We've had 84 pages of dog-related nonsense when really you only need to understand the following simple rules.

Five Rules of Cat

1. We're in charge.

2. See rule 1.

3. Why are you still here?

4. It's not like we even need a 4th rule.

5. Are you a dog?

Dogs and Squirrels

We have already mentioned these animals in previous chapters, but it feels appropriate to better prepare you for combat with these outrageous creatures.

Often working together in gangs, these cheeky animals delight in tormenting us. Their springy hopping action across the ground, combined with their flag-like tail, makes it seem as if they are taunting us.

But it is a rare dog that has ever been able to catch one. Their ability to go instantly vertical, just like cats, ensures that no matter how fast we run when locked on target, we never get close enough to catch them.

There is a legend of one dog – a fabled ancestor of old – who once managed to nip the end of a squirrel's tail, as his acorn-snaffling prey scampered up a fir tree.

He was immediately promoted to Colonel Lord High Marshal of the Squirrel Patrol and was henceforth known as

General Tailsnatch

Anatomy of a Squirrel

Beady eyes *for spotting approaching ninja hounds*

Fuzzy multi-directional sonar array

Flamboyant butt flag *for balance*

Nimble paws *to manipulate food or make obscene gestures*

Tree crampons *to easily evade pursuit*

Powerful leg muscles *to evade gnashing jaws in a single frustrating bound*

Dogs and Sheep

**Why is it that when some dogs chase sheep
they are rewarded and respected, but when the
vast majority of us do it, we may get shot?**

There is something so appealing about sending a flock of
sheep fleeing madly across a field with just a simple bark.

Sheep are our favourite field animals and they really
understand how to play the game of *chase*.

Unfortunately, humans don't like it when we join
in, and put us on the lead if we are anywhere
near our woolly friends (unless for some reason,
we are border collies. Humans are weird!).

There are many times when we question whether
sheep are our intellectual equals. They seem unable
to make independent decisions and will follow
their comrades into the most ridiculous situations.
We have no idea what the flock they're doing.

Sometimes we dream of the different games we could
play with sheep if we were ever left alone with them
for long. All it needs is a little bit of co-ordination,
which is where the border collies come in.

We call them
the Baa Baa Olympics.

Sheep Games

1. Sheep Skittles

2. Sheep Jumping*

3. Sheep Dipping

as pioneered by Beagle Knievel.

Dogs and Horses

Anything larger than us should be treated with respect. It's a fairly safe rule of thumb when dealing with the rest of the animal kingdom*.

However, dogs and horses are often pictured as the two faithful companions to humans, and we don't think that's very fair.

Dogs are way better than horses. Just because the horse can carry a human long distances and only needs to eat grass doesn't make it equal.

After all, we provide comfort and cuddles. We are the human's hot water bottle and keep them warm. We entertain humans with our antics and warn them of danger.

Who got domesticated first, buddy?

*especially when they have metal shoes.

Dogs v Horses: Pros and Cons.

Horse Pros

Can eat on the hoof.

Can support
human's weight.

Provides manure
for gardens.

Horse Cons

Doesn't fit on the couch.

Humans need equipment
to communicate
with horse.

Hard to lift up.

Dog Pros

Improves human's
mental health.

Provides security detail.

Eats poop.

Dog Cons

There are no cons.

The
Literary
Dog

A Dog's Serenity

Dog grant me the serenity

To accept the plates I cannot lick;

Courage to chase the squirrels I can;

And wisdom to know the difference.

Living one meal at a time;

Enjoying one tummy rub at a time;

Accepting grooming as the pathway to cuddles;

Taking, as we do, this weird human world

As it is, not as we would have it;

Trusting that they will make walks long

If we surrender to their leads;

So that we may be really quite happy in this life

And supremely happy with owner

Forever and ever in the kitchen.

Woof.

The Classics All Dogs Should Read

Jeeves and Woofster
P.G. Wodehouse

Greatest Dalmatians
Charles Dickens

Fetch-22
Joseph Heller

The Dogyssey
Homer

The Tail of Two Setters
Charles Dickens
(It was the bark of times and the woof of times)

Far from the Howling Crowd
Thomas Hardy

To Kill A Mockingcat
Harper Lee

Bad Boy and Punishment
Fyodor Dostoevsky

The Call of The Wild
Jack London

To The Doghouse
Virginia Woolf

Tess of the Dobermans
Thomas Hardy

One Flew Over The Cockapoo's Nest
Ken Kesey

Nineteen Eighty-Paw
George Orwell

Grapes of Ruff
John Steinbeck

The Count of Monte Shih tzu
Alexander Dumas

War and Leash
Leo Tolstoy

Hairy Tales

The Three Little Pigs

A triumphant tale of how a noble wolf manages
to eat two thirds of three little pigs.

Little Red Riding Hood

Noble wolf with very big teeth, persecuted
by a scarlet, woodland trespasser.

The Boy Who Cried Wolf

And why wouldn't he? He was merely drawing
attention to our lupine magnificence.

The Twelve Dogs of Christmas

Twelve Labradors a-leaping

Eleven Lhasa apsos dancing

Ten pointers pointing

Nine Dalmatians spotting

Eight mastiffs fighting

Seven schnausers swimming

Six greyhounds running

Five golden retrievers

Four cockapoos

Three French bulldogs

Two bassett hounds

And a poodle in a pear tree

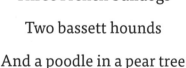

If
by Ruffyard Kibbling

If you can keep your head when all about you
Are losing theirs and blaming it on you;
If you can trust yourself when all dogs doubt you,
But make allowance for their doubting too;
If you can wait and not be tired by waiting,
Or, being lied about, don't deal in lies,
Or, being hated, don't give way to hating,
And yet don't look too good, nor bark too wise:

If you can dream – and not make dreams your human;
If you can think – and not make thoughts your aim;
If you can meet with Owner and Groomer
And treat those two humans just the same;
If you can bear to hear the woofs you've spoken
Twisted by cats to make a trap for paws,
Or watch the things you gave your life to broken,
And stoop and build'em up with wornout claws:

If you can make one heap of all your winnings
And risk it on one turn of tug-of-war,
And lose, and start again at your beginnings
And never breathe a word about your jaw;
If you can force your heart and nerve and sinew
To serve your turn long after they are gone,
And so hold on when there is nothing in you
Except the Lead which says to you: 'Hold on!'

If you can woof with crowds and keep your virtue,
Or howl with Kings – nor lose the common touch;
If neither cats nor loving owners can hurt you;
If all dogs count with you, but none too much;
If you can fill the unforgiving minute
With sixty seconds' snacks all eaten up –
Yours is the garden, and everything that's in it,
And – which is more – you'll be a good Boy, my pup!

On
the Origin of Species

BY MEANS OF NATURAL SELECTION,

OR THE PRESERVATION OF ~~FAVOURED RACES~~ DOGS IN THE STRUGGLE FOR LIFE

by Snarls Darwin, M.A.,

Fellow of the P.A.W.S, B.O.N.E, Wolf Squad, Etc., Societies

Author of 'Journal of Researches During
H.M.S. Beagle's Voyage Round the World'

LONDON:
JACK RUSSELL, ALBEMARLE STREET.
1859.

DETAILED CONTENTS.
ON THE ORIGIN OF SPECIES.

INTRODUCTION

VARIATION UNDER DOMESTICATION
Or how dogs perfect their human's behaviour

VARIATION UNDER NATURE
Or how dogs ensure survival of the
fittest in a Cat Eat Dog world

STRUGGLE FOR EXISTENCE
Or how dogs face a 'paw'-city of treats

NATURAL SELECTION
Or how to use those puppy dog eyes –
work them, work them hard!

LAWS OF VARIATION
Or adapting your human's environment to suit you

INSTINCT
Or always sleep with one eye open
and *never* trust a squirrel

HYBRIDISM
Or everyone's a doodle these days

GEOGRAPHICAL DISTRIBUTION
Or we're bloody everywhere

RECAPITULATION AND CONCLUSION
Or how dogs have taken over the
world (largely unopposed)!

Famous Doggie Phrases

All I need to make a comedy is a park, a
policeman and a pretty poodle.

Chihuahua Chaplin.

Mamma may have, papa may have, but God
bless the dog that's got his own.

Bulldog Holiday

A door is what a dog is perpetually on the wrong side of.

Dogden Gnash

The dog is a gentleman; I hope to go
to his heaven, not man's.

Bark Twain

There is no love sincerer than the love of food.

George St Bernard Shaw

And so to bed... and naps...

 Spaniel Pepys

The hills are alive with the sound of barking,
With howls they have yowled for a thousand years.
The hills fill my heart with the sound of barking,
My heart wants to howl ev'ry yowl it hears.

Oscar Howlerstein

A lick is a lovely trick designed by nature to stop
whines when barking becomes superfluous.

 Ingrid Barkman

Dogs in Shakespeare

Cry havoc and let slip the dogs of war!

Julius Caesar Act 3, Scene 1

I had rather hear my dog bark at a crow,
than a man swear he loves me.

Much Ado About Nothing Act 1, Scene 1

Thou call'st me dog before thou hadst a cause,
But since I am a dog, beware my fangs.

Merchant of Venice Act 3, Scene 3

Tao for Dogs

He who holds his head up high, steps in dog poop.

Every dog has beauty, but not everyone sees it.

**Choose a dog you love, and you'll never
be alone a day in your life.**

**A superior dog is modest in his barks
but exceeds in his tummy rubs.**

If you bow at all, bow low.

Collective Nouns of Dogs

A **Rorshak**
of Damalatians

A **drag**
of huskies

A **hairball**
of Labradors

An **enthusiam**
of golden retrievers

A **'You What, Mate?'**
of boxers

A **catwalk**
of poodles

A **jobsworth**
of Alsatians

A **swarm**
of Chihuahuas

A **trundle**
of dachshund

A **hyperactivity**
of border terriers

A **cacophony**
of Jack Russells

A **neurosis**
of greyhounds

The Cultured Dog

A Doggy Declaration of Independence

We hold these truths to be self-evident, that all dogs are created equal, that they are endowed by their Fore-Wolf with certain unalienable Rights, that among these are Food, Walkies and the pursuit of Tummy Rubs.

Universal Declaration

All dogs are born free and equal in dignity and rights.

Every dog has the right to food,
walkies and security of home.

Every dog has the right to be let off the
lead, providing it is safe to do so.

Every dog has the right to own toys
alone as well as share them.

Every dog has the right to worship whatever human
they desire, especially those practiced in tummy rubs.

# of Canine Rights

Every dog has the right to share woofs, barks and howls.

Every dog has the right to meet with other dogs,
providing they do so at Level 4 and below.

Every dog has the right to attend puppy training,
either in class or individually by their human.

Every dog has the right to sleep, play and have fun.

Every dog has the right to be presumed innocent until
proven guilty, especially in the case of missing snacks.

Shih Tzu's Art of Squirrel War

WOOF!
WOOF!
WOOF!
WOOF!

WOOF!
WOOF!
WOOF!
WOOF!

> Supreme excellence consists of breaking
> the enemy's resistance without fighting.

> In the midst of chaos,
> there is also opportunity.

> When you move, fall
> like a thunderbolt.

All warfare is based upon deception.

If he is superior in strength, evade him.

Ponder and deliberate, before you make a move.

Famous Doggy Battles

The Battle of Waterbowl
A battle between the poodle, Napoleon Boneapart
and the bulldog, Duke of Smellington.

The Scuffle of Agincourt
When a brave bunch of old English sheepdogs
used their superior knowledge of stick-throwing
to defeat a pack of rebellious poodles.

The Battle of Hastings
When a group of heroic pugs battled
a swarm of bees in a hayfield.

The Battle of Thermopuppy
When the Spartan rovers defended the Gates
of Fire from the Persian cat horde.

The Siege of Yorkietown
When a brave battalion of Yorkshire terriers held out
against a force of numerically superior feral cats.

The Battle of the Bulge
The story of an overweight Chihuahua's
battle with his addiction to treats.

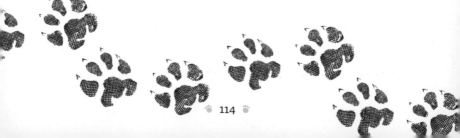

The Trojan Hound

Before the Trojan Horse, the Greeks had a lesser-known, but ultimately unsuccessful plan.

The Trojan Hound.

The Greeks left the wooden hound outside the gates of Troy, but after the Trojans took it inside the city, it immediately wanted to go back outside again.

Famous Dogs
Throughout History

Barchimedes

The first canine mathematician who spent most of his time working on circles, which many mistook for him chasing his tail.

Woofrow Wilson

Our highest political office, President of the Dog Nation, was held by Woofrow Wilson, during a period of extreme tension between our nation and our heriditary enemy, the Feline Empire. He came up with the famous political catchphrase, 'Better dog, than mog!'

Heel Armstrong

Dogs travel far and wide, not least, Heel Armstrong, who was one of the first dogs to walk on the moon. He is most famous for delivering the immortal line, 'This is one small step for a spaniel, one giant treat for dog kind.'

Indiana Bones

A fearless explorer pooch, whose dog-devil adventures are depicted in the famous movie, Raiders of the Lost Bark.

Bark Twain

A famous literary hound, who upon being found with peanut butter all over his face, famously said, 'The reports of my pantry raiding have been greatly exaggerated.'

Barking Luther King

Famously said, 'I had a dream. Of rabbits..... And running.... And running.... And running...'

The Rolling Bones

The first rock band in dog history, whose global fame was only eclipsed by super group, The Beagles.

The Woofragettes

These dogs fought for dogs' woofrage – our ability to have a say in how the humans treat us. In conjunction with the characters in the next few pages, they have made a huge difference in the level of comfort in our homes.

Dogs on Screen

Every once in a while, some of us are chosen to promote our species on the TV. These brave and hard-working hounds deal with ridiculous situations daily in order to demonstrate our bravery, kindness and loyalty to the human race. Don't think it has gone unnoticed that some directors deliberately choose to put their canine stars in jeopardy to elicit a strong emotional response from their audience.

Here are some of our most successful marketeers.

5. Pongo and Perdita, 101 Dalmatians (1961 / 1996)

The two stars of a bone-chilling horror movie, where their children are stalked by the monstrous child murderer, Cruella de Ville.

4. Frank the Pug, Men In Black (1997–2019)

Poor Frank was constantly surrounded by the freakish twisted forms of the humans of New York. Oh, there were some aliens too, but they aren't half as weird.

3. Bruiser (Chihuahua), Legally Blonde (2001–2003)

Bruiser had the most ridiculous costume changes – always having to wear pink. Every one knows that Chihuahuas are born for turquoise.

2. Lassie, The Lassie Movies (1943–2005)

Lassie is our finest Shakespearean actor. Although, for some reason, the stupid kids always seemed to think her magnificent soliloquies were saying that someone was stuck down a well.

1. Toto (Cairn terrier), The Wizard of Oz (1939)

Toto... we should pause to pay our respect... was one of the first, and greatest canine actors. To be clear, he was perfectly well aware that he and Dorothy weren't in Kansas anymore. Either that, or they'd suffered a traumatic head injury.

Hollywoof Legends

We have our own cinematic entertainment too, where we enjoy films with slightly different plotlines to the human versions of these blockbusters.

1. Jaws

The tale of two bitter rivals, a Doberman and a Rottweiler competing in the International Bite Strength Championships.

2. Reservoir Dogs

A pair of Pomeranians go for a swim.

3. The Deer Hunter

A training film for larger dogs, delivered by Fluffy the Chihuahua.

4. Close Encounters of the Third Kind

A harrowing portrayal of a dog who narrowly missed being scarred for life by a cat.

5. Up

A good-natured film reminding us that sometime it's better to leave squirrels alone.

6. Gone With The Wind

A tragic tale of old age and creeping bad smells.

7. Braveheart

Loyalty, courage, and stamina – all wrapped up
in a cockapoo's first trip to the groomer.

8. Beauty and the Beast

A light-hearted comedy about a spoiled French poodle
and a fierce Doberman learning to trust each other.

9. Slumdog Millionaire

A story of a dog from the ghetto who achieves success
on the TV gameshow, Who Wants To Be A Good Boy.

10. The Lion King

Know your enemy.

11. Groundhog Day

An educational film explaining why it's wrong for dogs
to shred the furniture when their human is out.

12. Rear Window

A slow-paced reprise of one dog's journey across America.

13. One Flew Over The Cuckoo's Nest

The story of a dog who leads an escape from
the pound the day before he is neutered.

14. The Silence of the Lambs

A heart-rending tale of a sheepchase gone wrong.

The World Wide Woof

Our humans started to spend large amounts of time glued to the small black rectangles they keep in their pocket, and often found out strange and alarming facts about the best way to train us into certain types of behaviour. (Peanut butter and clingfilm, we're looking at you!)

In our defence, it was important that we had something similar and so we developed the World Wide Woof.

Our main search engine, BEEGLE, allows us to discover new tactics against our feline enemies.

Humans flooded their internet with so many cat videos, the cats had to set up their own dedicated site to collect them all – it's called MEWTUBE.

Not only is there MEWTUBE, but there is also WIG WAG – a social media channel made of extremely short films. Older dogs prefer to use SNOUTBOOK, but it's going out of fashion with the younger pups.

Our main shopping woofsite is BARKAZON, but they are currently having a bit of an issue with their delivery drivers, as they seem reluctant to deliver to our front doors due to the noise. If you want particularly hard to obtain items, sometimes you need to travel to the BARK WEB, which is full of cat viruses.

We listen to our howling on DALMATIAN RADIO and have created long playlists that we listen to when our owners are out of the house.

The
Last
Bark

A few final words...

We hope that this guide to the doggie
world has given you a much better
understanding of how our world works.

There are lots of things you humans could do
better, but providing you remember the three most
important things in our lives (see pages 29–33 for a
reminder), give us plenty of affection and exercise,
we will pretty much do anything for you.

Just remember, we are your constant
companions – cats are supercilious interlopers,
and don't even get us started on horses.

See you round the campfire, humans!